Better
Before
Bigger

Practical Steps for Creating A Better And More Excellent Ministry

Dr. Terrance J. Gattis

ISBN: 978-1-7325735-0-5
Library of Congress Control Number: 2018952759

Printed in the United States of America

Dedication

This book is thankfully and gratefully dedicated to my wife Elaine.

I am so thankful and grateful that you are taking this journey through life with me. The Bible says "He who finds a wife finds a good thing" (Prov. 18:22). In my case, I have found a great thing! So I say from the bottom of my heart: Thank you and I love you!

Contents

Acknowledgments

Special thanks to….

Dr. Chike Akua

Dr. Thelma Gattis

Myron Gattis, Esq.

Troy Gattis

Ronnie Gattis

The Mt. Olive Church Family

Chapter 1

Introduction

"I planted, Apollos watered, but God gave the growth."

(1 Corinthians 3:6)

Introduction

"There is no secret sauce"

My wife is from the San Francisco Bay area in California. Several years ago, we traveled west for the Thanksgiving holiday to spend time with family and friends. While there, we ran into an old and dear friend of my wife who had recently planted a church. This young man had previously served in a large mega church. However, the Spirit of God led him to step out on faith and plant a new ministry. As a person who had previously planted a church, I truly understood where he was at that season of his life and ministry. So I sought to share my experiences and encourage him where I could.

But as we talked about all that he had learned from serving at his previous church, and how he planned to grow his new church, he made a statement that would stick with me for years: "There is no secret sauce". His point was that he had arrived at a place where he recognized that there is no magic bullet, or profound program, or secret strategy to grow a church. If there were such a magic bullet or sure-fire strategy, every church would be a mega ministry! He concluded that it was his task to do the best that he could with what he had, and trust that God would grow the church according to God's will, for only God can give the increase (1 Cor. 3:7).

Like many pastors and church leaders, my desire is to win as many souls as I can for Christ. For years, I have desired to do a great work for the Lord; a work that will lead to church growth and the ability to do ministry in ways that will save souls, transform lives, makes disciples, serve the community, and bring glory and honor to our God. But one day during my prayer time, I heard the Spirit say: "God will never give you more if you are not caring for what you already have". This took me back to my California conversation; to the notion that I must do the best that I can with what I already have. And as I strive to make what I have better, I can trust that God will increase what I have according to God's good and perfect will.

This principle and truth is clearly seen in the "Parable of the Talents" as recorded in Matthew's Gospel:

> "For it will be like a man going on a journey, who called his servants and entrusted to them his property. To one he gave five talents, to another two, to another one, to each according to his ability. Then he went away. He who had received the five talents went at once and traded with them, and he made five talents more. So also he who had the two talents made two talents more. But he who had received the one talent went and dug in the ground and hid

his master's money. Now after a long time the master of those servants came and settled accounts with them. And he who had received the five talents came forward, bringing five talents more, saying, 'Master, you delivered to me five talents; here, I have made five talents more.' His master said to him, 'Well done, good and faithful servant. You have been faithful over a little; I will set you over much. Enter into the joy of your master.' And he also who had the two talents came forward, saying, 'Master, you delivered to me two talents; here, I have made two talents more.' His master said to him, 'Well done, good and faithful servant. You have been faithful over a little; I will set you over much. Enter into the joy of your master.' He also who had received the one talent came forward, saying, 'Master, I knew you to be a hard man, reaping where you did not sow, and gathering where you scattered no seed, so I was afraid, and I went and hid your talent in the ground. Here, you have what is yours.' But his master answered him, 'You wicked and slothful servant! You knew that I reap where I have not sown and gather where I scattered no seed? Then you ought to have invested my money with the bankers, and at my coming I should have received what was my own with interest. So take the talent from him and give it to him who has the ten talents. For to everyone who has will more be given, and he will have an abundance. But from the one who has not, even what he has will be taken away." (Matt. 25:14-29)

As evident in the parable, the two who took what they had and worked to make it better, were blessed with more. However, the one who sat on what he had, and did nothing to improve it, ultimately lost what he had.

So what is the lesson so far? Here it is: "there is no secret sauce." There are no mysteries or quick recipes for church growth. What is true and what is clear is that the Lord has entrusted pastors and church leaders with the care of God's church. Our job is to take that which we have been entrusted and be intentional at making it better. And when we do our part to make our churches better, we put ourselves in position for God to make our churches bigger.

Over the next few chapters, I will share practical steps to help your church become better regardless of its size. The strategy is to give you the tools to evaluate your church from the outside to the inside (from the parking to the pew), and consider what you can do right now to have a better and more excellent ministry.

Specifically, we will look at how to make your buildings and grounds better, your ministries and programs better, your worship experience better, your servant-leaders better, and your messaging better. Please note that the tools and principles in this book will only work if you are honest with yourself and honest about your church. My prayer is that these prudent, practical, and biblically based principles will bless your ministry with a continuous spirit of excellence that will honor God and enable you to hear the Lord say, "Well done my good and faithful servant! You have been faithful over a little; so I will set you over much"!

Chapter 2

Get Your Mind Right

"Be transformed by the renewal of your mind."

(Romans 12:2)

Get Your Mind Right

I have been working with pastors and church leaders for some time now with respect to making their churches better. I have been blessed to do quite a few workshops with churches of various sizes and denominations. While the churches have differed in size and denomination, what is common is that, invariably, there are always a few people in the room who will doubt that their church can become better, needs to become better, or will ever become better. In a very real sense, they are bound to the status quo because the chains of doubt and apathy have shackled their minds.

Over the years, I have heard people say things like:

- Things are not that bad at our church, so this workshop is probably not necessary for us
- We do not have a lot of money and the changes that we need will cost more than we have
- We do not need to get better, we just need more people and for the current members to step up and do more
- We will never be able to do any more than we are doing so why even try
- We have been around for over one hundred years and what we are doing has worked and will continue to work
- As long as the preaching is good, that is all that matters

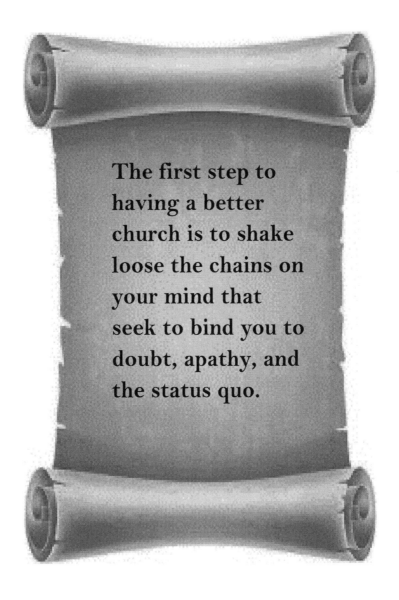

The first step to having a better church is to shake loose the chains on your mind that seek to bind you to doubt, apathy, and the status quo.

It is safe to say that it is not until you change your thinking and believe that you can become better, or believe that you need to become better, that you will take the steps to actually become better. It short, the road to change always begins with a change in our attitude and our thinking. The Bible says it this way, "Be transformed by the renewal of your mind" (Rom. 12:2). Thus, the first step to having a better church is to shake loose the chains on your mind that seek to bind you to doubt, apathy, and the status quo.

Consider the story of Shon Hopwood.[1] At the age of 23, Shon was sentenced to eleven years in federal prison for bank robbery. While in prison, he got a job at the law library. For the first six months in the library, he did not read any of the law books because they seemed too big and intimidating. He was being hindered by apathy and fear. But one day he motivated himself to change his thinking. He pushed aside his fear and decided to open a law book.

After a while, Shon became a "jail house lawyer", writing briefs and appeals for fellow inmates. And it is here where Shon's life took an amazing turn. From prison, he wrote two briefs that ended up before the U.S. Supreme Court, a feat that most lawyers never accomplish. After getting out of prison, Shon went on to graduate from law school and practice law, and he has even become a law professor at Georgetown Law School. All of this happen in Shon's life simply because he got his mind right – he set himself free from the chains of doubt and apathy. He changed his thinking and decided to use what he had to better himself and those around him.

Likewise, there has to come a point when you shift your thinking. There has to come a point when you break the chains of doubt and apathy. There are people who need your help. There are people who need to experience the love of Christ. And when you are willing to move beyond the status quo, God will open new doors for you and enable your ministry to reach more people in your community.

Mediocrity Is A Mindset

The year was 1992. I had just moved to the Atlanta area and was driving around the city in the effort to become acquainted and acclimated with my new surroundings. As I drove through the various neighborhoods, I was listening to the radio. As I listened, the radio host started talking about how important it is to strive for greatness in your life. She said that we must work hard to be the best that we can be. As she spoke, she said something that I never forgot: "What you tolerate will become your standard".

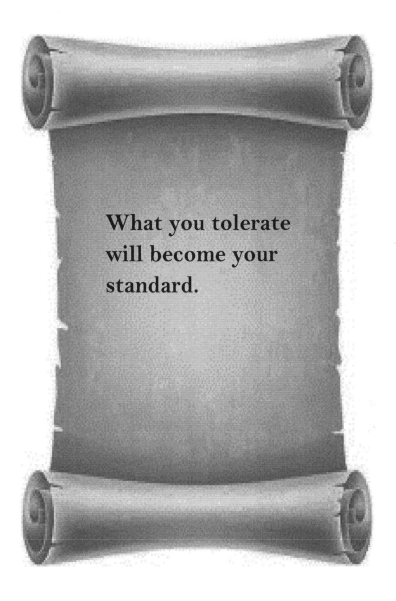

What you tolerate
will become your
standard.

If you think about it, this statement is amazingly true. If you tolerate "Cs" in school, you will become a C student. If you tolerate dysfunction in your relationships, dysfunction will become a normative aspect of your relationships. If you tolerate apathy, you will get comfortable where you are and you will never challenge the status quo. And if you tolerate a mediocre ministry, a mediocre ministry is what you will have. What you tolerate becomes your standard.

When you get down to it, mediocrity is a mindset. To be mediocre, by definition, means to be of low quality or not very good. All too often, we allow our minds to accept and grow comfortable with low quality and mediocrity because we either do not believe that we have the resources to do any better, we do not see the value of doing and becoming better, or we do not believe that we are able to do any better. Thus, we accept things as they are and we begin to believe that something is better than nothing. We accept mediocrity because we believe that we do not have what it takes to make things better.

We can see this mindset playout in the early portion of Gideon's story:

> "And the Lord turned to him and said, "Go in this might of yours and save Israel from the hand of Midian; do not I send you?" And he said to him,

"Please, Lord, how can I save Israel? Behold, my clan is the weakest in Manasseh, and I am the least in my father's house." And the Lord said to him, "But I will be with you, and you shall strike the Midianites as one man." (Judg. 6:14-16)

When we meet Gideon in this text, we find him at a low place in his life. He is threshing wheat in a winepress in a cave because he is afraid that the army of the Midianites might show up and take everything that he has. But things are about to change for Gideon and for God's people. God is about to use Gideon to do great things. God is about to use him to defeat the army of the Midianites.

Notice that when the angel speaks to Gideon, the angel does not address him by his name. Rather the angel addresses him by what he shall be – "mighty". God instructs Gideon to go forth in the strength that he already has. God was going to bless what he already had to save Israel out of the hands of the Midianites.

However, because Gideon's mind was in the wrong place, he began to do what far too many of us have done, he begins to talk himself out of doing and becoming what God would have him to do and become. First, he allowed his mind to focus on his communal shortcomings, for he lamented that his clan was the weakest in Manasseh. He then shifts his focus to his personal shortcomings, for he laments that he is the least in his father's house. But in his lamenting, what he forgot is that it was not just about him. It was also about the God who was for him and with him.

As pastors and church leaders, we need to keep in mind that God's power is made perfect in our weaknesses (2 Cor. 12:9). It does not matter how small we are. It does not matter the size of our bank accounts. It does not matter how many people attend our church. When we are willing to use what we have by faith, God's power connects with our effort to produce great fruit for the Kingdom of God - fruit that will last! We just have to believe in our hearts and minds that God's Word is true: "We can do all things through Christ who strengthens us" (Phil. 4:13).

In their book, *The Five Start Church*, Stan Toler and Alan Nelson make it clear that "quality starts as a mind-set and, like our faith, ends up with tangible fruit."[2] What Toler and Nelson mean is that excellence and the pursuit of quality has nothing to do with a plethora of resources, and everything to do with an attitude and a mindset that refuses to settle for low quality, disorder, and messiness. The bottom line is that you can have a nice house even if your house is not a mansion. You can have a nice car even if your car is not a Mercedes-Benz. And you can have an excellent and quality ministry even if your ministry is not a mega ministry. It all begins with a mindset that says, "I'm willing to do the best that I can with what I have and I refuse to settle for mediocrity".

To Whom Much is Given, Much Is Required

As a pastor and a church leader, you have been entrusted with much; you have been entrusted with the responsibility to care for the church of Jesus Christ. When God gives us much, much is required. This truth is seen in marvelous manner in the story where Joshua allocates land to the tribes of Ephraim and Manasseh:

> "Then the people of Joseph spoke to Joshua, saying, "Why have you given me but one lot and one portion as an inheritance, although I am a numerous people, since all along the Lord has blessed me?" And Joshua said to them, "If you are a numerous people, go up by yourselves to the forest, and there clear ground for yourselves in the land of the Perizzites and the Rephaim, since the hill country of Ephraim is too narrow for you." The people of Joseph said, "The hill country is not enough for us. Yet all the Canaanites who dwell in the plain have chariots of iron, both those in Beth-shean and its villages and those in the Valley of Jezreel." Then Joshua said to the house of Joseph, to Ephraim and Manasseh, "You are a numerous people and have great power. You shall not have one allotment

only, but the hill country shall be yours, for though it is a forest, you shall clear it and possess it to its farthest borders. For you shall drive out the Canaanites, though they have chariots of iron, and though they are strong." (Jos. 17:14-18)

The book of Joshua can best be described as a report that makes it clear that God is a promise keeper. Way back in the book of Genesis, God promised Abraham that the land of Canaan would be the Promised Land for the decedents of Abraham. After many years had passed, the promise of God had come to fruition, for God's people had finally taken possession of the promise land. God had done what God had promised.

As pastors and leaders we have to know for ourselves that God is a promise keeper. Bringing about change within a church can get hard sometimes. But no matter how hard things get, we can draw strength from standing firm on the promises of God. God promised, for example, to never leave us nor forsake us (Heb. 13:5). So as we work to make our churches better, we are not working alone, God is with us!

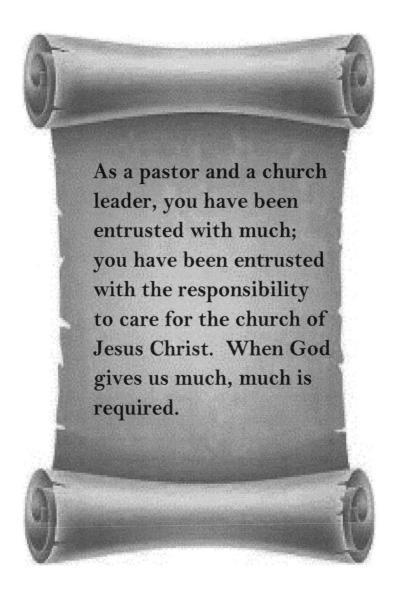

As a pastor and a church leader, you have been entrusted with much; you have been entrusted with the responsibility to care for the church of Jesus Christ. When God gives us much, much is required.

After taking possession of the land, Joshua began to divide and distribute the land among the tribes of Israel as God had instructed. But in chapter seventeen of the text, we find that a problem has arisen. The decedents of Joseph, the tribes of Ephraim and Manasseh, had issues with the portion of land that they had received. Because they were a numerous people, they wanted a larger portion of land. So, Joshua provides the remedy for their problem, "Go up to the hill portion of the land and clear it for yourselves" (v. 15). Joshua is encouraging them to take what they had and make it better. They had been given much, and now much would be required.

On the one hand, to make what they had better would require them to put in some work. Here is a news flash for you: while salvation is free, there are some blessings that will cost you something. Some blessings will require that you make some sacrifices and put in some work. Joshua instructed them to get up and clear the land themselves. Others would not do it for them. If they wanted their land to be better, they would have to put in some work and make it better.

Over the years, I have discovered that too many people are what I have come to call "lottery minded". They want to put in a little work and get back a whole lot in return; they want to put in one dollar and get back one million. But what this text is tailored to teach us, is that some blessings will require some time, effort, and hard work on our part. God wants to bring about positive change in your ministry; God wants to bless you with a harvest. But in order to get a harvest, you have to go to work and plant some seed. No seed, no harvest. No work, no change.

On the one hand, the people discovered that what they had been given would require them to put in some work. But on the other hand, they also discovered that what they had been given would require them to put up a fight. Within the context of their situation, there were opponents and adversaries in their way. An enemy was standing between them and the better situation that they were seeking. And because the enemy was armed with iron chariots, God's people did not think that they could overcome their opposition.

Here is another news flash: Enemies, adversaries, and opponents are not going to just sit back and let you bring about those changes that will edify and build up the church of Jesus Christ. Jesus did tell Peter, "Upon this rock I will build my church, and the gates of hell shall not prevail against it" (Matt. 16:18). In other words, while hell will not prevail, hell will put up a fight. Adversaries will try to stand between you and the better that you are seeking.

To be sure, you are going to have to fight to make your ministry better. But somethings are worth fighting for. The vision that God has given you is worth fighting for. The people who are being blessed and who will be blessed through your church are worth fighting for. The community that you serve is worth fighting for. The souls who will be saved and set free at your church are worth fighting for. So get ready to put up a fight.

But here is the good news: Since God is on our side, the battle is already won! Scripture reminds us that "weapons formed against us shall not proposer" (Isa. 54:17). Joshua obviously shared this sentiment, for he told the tribes of Ephraim and Manasseh to go up against the enemies in the hill country "for surely you can drive them out" (v. 18). Likewise, because God is with you, you will be able to drive out the adversaries and opponents who will stand in the way of progress at your church.

So, get your mind right. Shake loose the chains that are keeping you bound to apathy and the status quo. Moreover, be sure to move away from a mediocre mindset. Lastly, get ready to work and get ready to fight. God has entrusted you with much, and when much is given much is required. In the context of your church, what is required is that you do what you can, while you can, to make your ministry better.

Study Questions

1. What is your main take away from this chapter?

2. What are some of the barriers that might be hindering you from making your church better?

3. Do you see yourself in the Gideon story (Judges 6)? If so, how?

Chapter 3

Better Buildings & Grounds

"I intend to build a house for the name of the Lord
my God."

(1 Kings 5:5)

Better Buildings & Grounds

A few years ago, a good friend invited me to lunch. He had been raving about a great hamburger place and we decided to go there for some afternoon food and fellowship. He picked me up at my office and we began the journey to the restaurant. As we got close, he turned to me and said, "Now, I need to give you a heads-up about this hamburger spot. It is a hole-in-the-wall. It is grimy, it is dingy, and it is not the greatest looking place. But don't worry, the burgers are great". Needless to say, everything that he said about the restaurant was true. It did not look appealing at all. But I have to admit, the burgers were delicious!

If you think about it, there are places of worship that fall into the same category as the aforementioned restaurant – churches were the "Word" is great, but the location is uninviting and unappealing. Some time ago, I was invited to preach at a church. When I arrived, I was surprised and disappointed at the condition of the church. From the outside to the inside, the church was not very appealing.

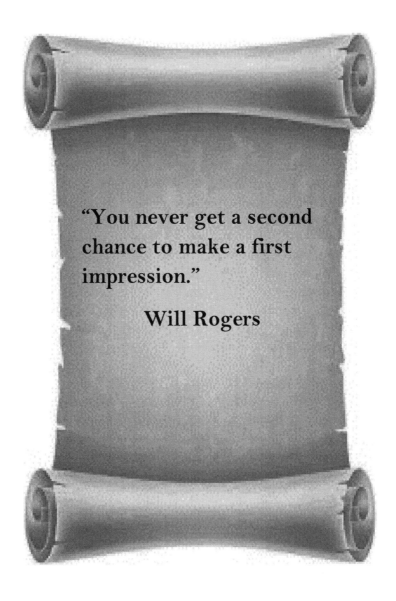

"You never get a second chance to make a first impression."

Will Rogers

Externally, the grass was not cut and weeds were growing everywhere. Trash was strewn across the lawn of the church, and the paint on the building was old and peeling. Internally, the carpets were old and dingy, the bathrooms were not clean, and the sanctuary was poorly lit because blown light bulbs had not been replaced. While the church may have had positive things happening within the ministry, the building and grounds were not reflective of these positive things.

You Only Have One Shot To Make A Good Impression

The great Will Rogers once said, "You never get a second chance to make a first impression".[1] Author James P. Wind puts it this way, "Early impressions are hard to eradicate from the mind".[2] When people drive up to your church, or go into your church, what they see will influence their impression of your ministry. In fact, the physical presentation of our churches not only communicates our concern (or lack thereof) about the first impressions that people will have regarding our ministry, it also communicates our concern (or lack thereof) about the overall care of God's house. So, you have to ask yourself: what does your buildings and grounds say about your concern with first impressions and your concern about the overall care of God's house?

Before you answer this question, consider the narrative that documents the building of God's temple by King Solomon:

"So Solomon built the temple and completed it. He lined its interior walls with cedar boards, paneling them from the floor of the temple to the ceiling, and covered the floor of the temple with planks of juniper. He partitioned off twenty cubits at the rear of the temple with cedar boards from floor to ceiling to form within the temple an inner sanctuary, the Most Holy Place. The main hall in front of this room was forty cubits long. The inside of the temple was cedar, carved with gourds and open flowers. Everything was cedar; no stone was to be seen. He prepared the inner sanctuary within the temple to set the ark of the covenant of the Lord there. The inner sanctuary was twenty cubits long, twenty wide and twenty high. He overlaid the inside with pure gold, and he also overlaid the altar of cedar. Solomon covered the inside of the temple with pure gold, and he extended gold chains across the front of the inner sanctuary, which was overlaid with gold. So he overlaid the whole interior with gold. He also overlaid with gold the altar that belonged to the inner sanctuary.

One wing of the first cherub was five cubits long, and the other wing five cubits—ten cubits from wing tip to wing tip. The second cherub also measured ten cubits, for the two cherubim were identical in size and shape. The height of each cherub was ten cubits. He placed the cherubim inside the innermost room of the temple, with their wings spread out. The wing of one cherub touched one wall, while the wing of the other touched the other wall, and their wings touched each other in the middle of the room. He overlaid the cherubim with gold. On the walls all around the temple, in both the inner and outer rooms, he carved cherubim, palm trees and open flowers. He also covered the floors of both the inner and outer rooms of the temple with gold. For the entrance to the inner sanctuary he made doors out of olive wood that were one fifth of the width of the sanctuary. And on the two olive-wood doors he carved cherubim, palm trees and open flowers, and overlaid the cherubim and palm trees with hammered gold. In the same way, for the entrance to the main hall he made doorframes out of olive wood that were one fourth of the width of the hall. He also made two doors out of juniper wood, each having two leaves that turned in sockets. He carved cherubim, palm trees and open flowers on them and overlaid them with gold hammered evenly over the carvings. And he built the inner courtyard of three courses of dressed stone and one course of trimmed cedar beams. The foundation of the temple of the Lord was laid in the fourth year, in the month of Ziv. In the eleventh year in the month of Bul, the eighth month, the temple was finished in all its details according to its specifications. He had spent seven years building it." (1 Ki. 6:1-38)

When considering this text, a few things jump out right away. The attention to detail is something that is obvious and evident. Solomon was attentive to the height and width of certain things concerning the inner and the outer sanctuary. He was concerned with how the temple looked on the outside and the inside. Moreover, he was attentive to the materials that were used and how things were placed within the temple. To be sure, details mattered to Solomon. And it was his attention to detail that ensured that the temple would reflect a sense of quality and excellence.

The other aspect of Solomon's temple that jumps out is that it was a house that was built "for the Lord" (v2). The way the external part of the temple was built and cared for reflected a concern for the Lord. The way the internal part of the temple was built and cared for reflected a concern for the Lord. As Solomon surveyed the house that he was building, God was never far from his mind. Thus, every aspect of the temple was meant to bring glory and honor to God.

I believe the lesson to be learned from Solomon's temple is that the buildings and grounds of our churches matter. How our churches look on the outside and inside speaks to the message that we want to convey about our ministry, and speaks to our theology about how we should care for the house of God. Our buildings and grounds should engender a positive first impression and bring glory and honor to God. Not through a grand and opulent presentation, but rather through a presentation that reflects excellence, care, and a desire to honor God in every aspect of our ministry.

What About Your Buildings and Grounds?

It is prudent at this point to raise the relevant question again: What do the buildings and grounds of your church say about your ministry? What does it say about your concern with first impressions and your concern about the overall care of God's house? Write three to five words that would describe the first impressions of your church:

_____

_____

_____

To get a more qualitative analysis of your church's buildings and grounds, answer the following questions:

Circle your response:

1. Do Not Agree
2. Somewhat Agree
3. Agree
4. Strongly Agree
5. Not Applicable

External Area

Your landscaping is consistently maintained

1 2 3 4 5

You property is clean and generally free of litter and trash

1 2 3 4 5

The paint on your building is not old or peeling

1 2 3 4 5

Your marquee is visible and in good condition

1 2 3 4 5

The area has appropriate lighting

1 2 3 4 5

There is accessible and ample amounts of parking

1 2 3 4 5

Vehicles are monitored and are reasonably secure

1 2 3 4 5

Internal Area

Your lobby area is welcoming and clear of clutter

1 2 3 4 5

Your carpets and floors are clean and not worn

1 2 3 4 5

Your bathrooms are clean and in working order

1 2 3 4 5

Your hallways are illuminated and easily accessible

1 2 3 4 5

Your sanctuary is bright and well lit

1 2 3 4 5

The temperature in the building is consistently comfortable

1 2 3 4 5

There are signs that provide directional information

1 2 3 4 5

There is ample and comfortable seating

1 2 3 4 5

You have a written maintenance schedule for your church

1 2 3 4 5

What are some of the positive features about your current property?

_____

_____

_____

_____

_____

_____

_____

What is the most pressing area for improvement?

_____

_____

_____

_____

_____

_____

_____

_____

_____

What changes to your buildings and grounds would you like to make within the next twelve months?

_____

_____

_____

_____

_____

_____

_____

_____

_____

There are many more questions about your buildings and grounds about which you must consider. However, the intent of this exercise is to get you thinking about where you currently are in regard to the physical areas of your church, and the changes that you can incorporate to make your physical areas better.

Think about it. When you are looking for lodging when you travel, you probably are not looking to stay at Joe's motel on the side of the interstate. Rather, you are looking to stay at a five star hotel. A quality hotel that is well kept. A hotel that is appealing and inviting.

Likewise, your church should be a five star church. It should convey quality and excellence. It should be appealing and inviting. When your church is appealing and inviting, first-time visitors will have a better impression of your ministry. Moreover, when you honor God by taking care of God's house, God will bless your ministry in return.

In closing, consider this text from the prophetic book of Haggai:

> "Then the word of the Lord came through the prophet Haggai: "Is it a time for you yourselves to be living in your paneled houses, while this house remains a ruin? Now this is what the Lord Almighty says: "Give careful thought to your ways. You have planted much, but harvested little. You eat, but never have enough. You drink, but

never have your fill. You put on clothes, but are not warm. You earn wages, only to put them in a purse with holes in it." This is what the Lord Almighty says: "Give careful thought to your ways. Go up into the mountains and bring down timber and build my house, so that I may take pleasure in it and be honored," says the Lord. "You expected much, but see, it turned out to be little. What you brought home, I blew away. Why?" declares the Lord Almighty. "Because of my house, which remains a ruin, while each of you is busy with your own house." (Hag. 1:3-9)

It is not hard to see that God is not happy with how God's house was being treated. It appears that those who had the responsibility for caring for the house of God were not caring for it as they should. So God withholds His blessings. The people planted, but they harvested little. The people had drink, but they were never full. They put on clothes, but they were never warm. They earned money, but they could not hold on to the money that they earned. In short, satisfaction and blessings were escaping the people because they were not exercising excellent stewardship over God's house.

But when we invert the text, and look at it from a different point of view, it is not hard to see that God will bless those who take care of His house. If God's house was not in ruins, and if God had been pleased with the condition and care of the temple, it is safe to assume that the people would have been full, warm, and prosperous. It is safe to assume that if God's house was in order, the people would have reaped a harvest from all that they had planted.

As a pastor or church leader, I am confident that you want to reap a harvest within your ministry. If so, then be sure to put yourself in position to be blessed by doing all that you can to make God's house better. Be sure that the buildings and grounds of your church present a positive first impression for God's people, and that your overall care for God's house conveys your desire to bring glory and honor to God.

Study Questions

1. What is your main take away from this chapter?

2. What is your interpretation of Solomon's role in the building of God's temple? What about your role? Do you see yourself in Solomon?

3. What will be your biggest challenge when it comes to making your buildings and grounds better?

Chapter 4

Better Ministries & Programs

"For I was hungry and you gave me food…"
(Matthew 25:35)

Better Ministries & Programs

In 2005, I came across an article that truly resonated with me. It was an article written in the Washington Post by John W. Fountain that was entitled: "No Place for Me: I Still Love God, But I've Lost Faith in the Black Church".[1] I was a seminary student at the Candler School of Theology when I first read this article. I was in school working hard and investing a lot of time and money to prepare for ministry in the Black Church, and here was somebody writing about losing faith in the Black Church. To be sure, I was highly interested in what Mr. Fountain had to say, and what I read had a profound impact on how I would ultimately view ministry.

In the article, Fountain says, "I now feel disconnected. I am disconnected. Not necessarily from God, but from the church. What happened? Probably the same thing that has happened to thousands, if not tens of thousands, of African American men who now file into coffee shops or bowling alleys or baseball stadiums on Sundays instead of heading to church, or who lose themselves in the haze of mowing the lawn or waxing their cars. Somewhere along the way, for us, for me, the church -- the collective of black churches of the Christian faith, regardless of denomination -- lost its meaning, its relevance."

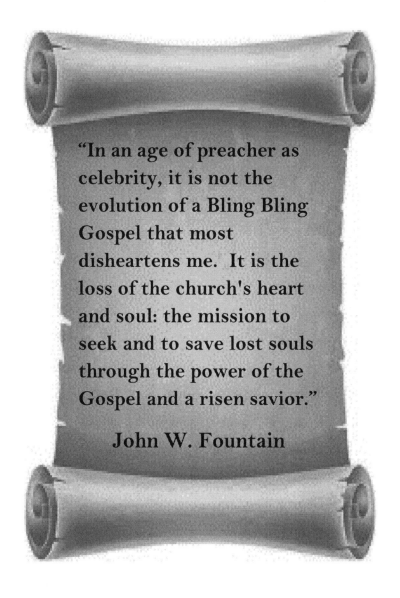

"In an age of preacher as celebrity, it is not the evolution of a Bling Bling Gospel that most disheartens me. It is the loss of the church's heart and soul: the mission to seek and to save lost souls through the power of the Gospel and a risen savior."

John W. Fountain

Fountain goes on to say, "In an age of preacher as celebrity, it is not the evolution of a Bling Bling Gospel that most disheartens me. It is the loss of the church's heart and soul: the mission to seek and to save lost souls through the power of the Gospel and a risen savior. As the homicide toll in black neighborhoods has swelled, I've wondered why churches or pastors have seldom taken a stand or ventured beyond the doors of their sanctuaries to bring healing and hope to the community -- whether to stem the tide of violence and drugs, or to help cure poverty and homelessness or any number of issues that envelop ailing black communities."

If you think about it, what Fountain is questioning are the ministries and programs of the church. Are the ministries relevant? Are the programs meeting the real needs of the people within the church and beyond the walls of the church? Is the church transforming lives? Are the ministries and programs serving the lost, the least, the left behind, and the left out?

The Church Is Called To Do Ministry

The work and ethic of Jesus Christ makes it clear that the church is called to do ministry. Through the church's programs and ministries, and through the power of the Holy Spirit, lives will be transformed. The Bible clearly addresses the mandate for ministry, for a careful exploration of Scripture reveals that: 1) the church is called to reach out to those in need; 2) Jesus, through the power of the Holy Spirit, will bring about transformation to those in need; and 3) God will provide the resources necessary to serve those in need.

In Matthew's Gospel, we clearly see the mandate that supports the notion that we are called to reach out and help those in need:

> "Then the King will say to those on his right, 'Come, you who are blessed by my Father, inherit the kingdom prepared for you from the foundation of the world. For I was hungry and you gave me food, I was thirsty and you gave me drink, I was a stranger and you welcomed me, I was naked and you clothed me, I was sick and you visited me, I was in prison and you came to me." (Matt. 25:34-36)

These verses give voice to the reality of a divine edict that bids us to reach out and care for those in need. Christians are called to feed the hungry, to provide clothing to those in need, to care for the sick, and to visit those in prison. Moreover, when we care for those in need, the Bible says that we will be considered "blessed" and will be rewarded for doing what God has called us to do (Matt. 25:34).

The notion of doing ministry that seeks to serve God's people is also supported by Scriptures beyond the Gospels. For example, in the Epistle of James, the writer poses a profound question:

> "What good is it, my brothers, if a man claims
> to have faith but has no deeds?" (Jam. 2:14)

The writer of James follows this question with the following observation:

> "Suppose a brother or sister is without clothes
> and daily food. If one of you says to him, "Go,
> I wish you well; keep warm and well fed," but
> does nothing about his physical needs, what
> good is it? In the same way, faith by itself, if it
> is not accompanied by action, is dead." (Jam.
> 2:15-17)

The writer is affirming what faith in action looks like. Thus, when we care for those in our church and in our local community, we are "doing" what faith in Jesus ought to compel us to do - to take action and help someone in need.

Additionally, through the power of the Holy Spirit, transformation will occur for those in need. The power of the Holy Spirit will connect with our ministries and programs to bring about positive change for those we serve. The Bible confirms that "if anyone is in Christ, he is a new creation; the old has gone, the new has come!" (2 Cor. 5:17).

We see this claim supported throughout the Gospels with respect to Jesus' efforts to transform the lives of individuals. For example, in John's Gospel Jesus restores the sight of a man who was born blind (Jn. 9:1-6). Yet, in restoring the man's sight, Jesus also spiritually enriched the man's capacity to believe in Christ (Jn. 9:35-38). Thus, when the church engages in ministry (i.e. to feed a person who is hungry), the heart of the individual becomes more open to receive the love and salvation of Christ.

The notion of Jesus as transformer can also be seen in the Gospels. For example, Matthew reports that Jesus "entered the temple area and drove out all who were buying and selling there. He overturned the tables of the money changers and the benches of those selling doves" (Matt. 21:12). M. Eugene Boring argues that Jesus overturned the tables because the community had "profaned the Temple by making it into a price-gouging business enterprise."[2]

Actually, the poor were being taken advantage of in their efforts to purchase the animals that were required for their sacrifices. Hence, Jesus is transforming the community by challenging the practices that had negatively affected the poor. As we seek to follow Christ, the church must be willing to confront and seek to transform those institutions and practices in the local community that underserve, or otherwise try to take advantage of, the poor and marginalized.

Lastly, we must recognize and believe that God will provide the resources necessary to engage in those ministries and programs that will bless God's people. The old Baptist saying: "the Lord will provide," is supported, for example, in the Old Testament book of Leviticus, where God tells the people:

> "When you reap the harvest of your land, do not reap to the very edges of your field or gather the gleanings of your harvest. Do not go over your vineyard a second time or pick up the grapes that have fallen. Leave them for the poor and the alien. I am the LORD your God." (Lev. 19:9-10)

These verses make it clear that through the harvest, the Lord is providing what the people need. Hence, while the Lord does bless God's people with resources, a portion of these resources are given so that we can serve others. God is the source of every resource that we have, and through these resources God calls us to provide for those in need.

The theological claim that God will provide what we need to care for others is also supported in the New Testament. For example, in Luke's Gospel we find that Jesus is concerned with the needs of the multitude that has gathered before Him (Lk. 9:13). Ordering the people to sit, Jesus served the people by providing food for five thousand people by divinely multiplying two fish and five loaves of bread (Lk. 9:16). Thus, the text makes it clear that when we are willing to use what we have to meet the concerns of God's people, God will provide the resources that are needed via divine multiplication. In short, God will take our little and turn it into much!.

What About Your Ministries and Programs?

According to Tom Frank, a congregation is "a people of God called together and gifted for ministry in a particular place."[3] So what are the ministries and programs currently occurring in your particular place?

Take a moment to write down some of the ministries and programs at your church:

_____

_____

_____

_____

_____

_____

To get a more qualitative analysis of your church's programs and ministries, answer the following questions:

Circle your response:

1. Do Not Agree

2. Somewhat Agree

3. Agree

4. Strongly Agree

5. Not Applicable

Ministries and Programs

Your ministries and programs are meeting needs in your church

1 2 3 4 5

Your ministries and programs are meeting needs beyond the walls of your church

1 2 3 4 5

You have added new ministries or programs in the last year

1 2 3 4 5

Your ministries and programs leaders are passionate and trained

1 2 3 4 5

Your ministries and programs foster transformation and change

1 2 3 4 5

You evaluate the effectiveness of your ministries and programs

1 2 3 4 5

You discontinue those ministries and programs that are no longer effective

1 2 3 4 5

What programs and ministries are currently working well?

_____

_____

_____

_____

_____

_____

_____

_____

What programs and ministries are ripe for improvement?

_____

_____

_____

_____

_____

_____

_____

What new programs and ministries would you like to add in the next twelve months?

_____

_____

_____

_____

_____

_____

_____

I have learned over the years that it does not take many people or a great deal of money to do transformative work through your ministries and programs. Actually, a few can accomplish much for God's people. I experienced this first hand during my pastorate. Prior to being called to my current church, I served as the Pastor of Bethesda Baptist Church in Decatur, GA. Bethesda was a "planted" church that I founded and organized in April, 2006.

In 2009, with a membership of less than fifty people, we started a meals on wheels type of program that delivered more than two thousand pounds of food twice per month to people in need within the community. In the same year, we opened the "House of Grace" healthcare clinic. The clinic provided free primary care services (physical exams, lab services, and screenings), as well as free prevention care services (nutrition classes, smoking cessation, and weight and stress management classes) to the uninsured in the community. Additionally, the clinic provided limited prescription drug assistance to those in need.

This experience proved that a few can do much when God is on your side. Moreover, it proved that through the power of the Holy Spirit, the church can meet the needs of those within the church and beyond the walls of the church, and can change lives in the process. Lastly, it proved that God will always provide the resources necessary for the programs and ministries that seek to faithfully serve the community. So, as you work to make your ministries and programs better, know that God will provide everything that you need to serve God's people.

Study Questions

1. What is your main take away from this chapter?

2. What do you think about John Fountains' statement at the beginning of the chapter? Do you agree with him?

3. What is your interpretation of Matthew 25:34 and James 2:15-17? Do these Scriptures change the way you see ministry?

Chapter 5

Better Worship Experiences

"Where the Spirit of the Lord is, there is freedom."
(2 Corinthians 3:17)

Better Worship Experiences

In Robert Franklin's work *Another Day's Journey: Black Churches Confronting the American Crisis*, he reminds us that the Sunday morning worship experience "seeks to facilitate a palpable sense of God's existence and love." [1] Through the contemporary and traditional worship experience, people are able to come into the very presence of God and encounter our Lord's liberating love. In truth, there is life-changing power in praise and worship and the overall experience of a Sunday morning worship celebration.

We have all had the experience of having to press our way to church on a Sunday morning. We thought about not even going to church. Maybe we were tired from a long workweek. Maybe we were feeling overwhelmed and weighted down by the problems and pressures of life. But we got up anyway, and made our way to the Lord's house.

Upon arrival, however, something changed. Hearing the Hammond organ, the drums, and the choir lifted our spirits. Hearing the preached Word encouraged our hearts and enlivened our hope. We began to feel revived and renewed, for we were transformed by the power of the Sunday morning worship service. It was this power that enabled us to leave the church feeling better than when we entered.

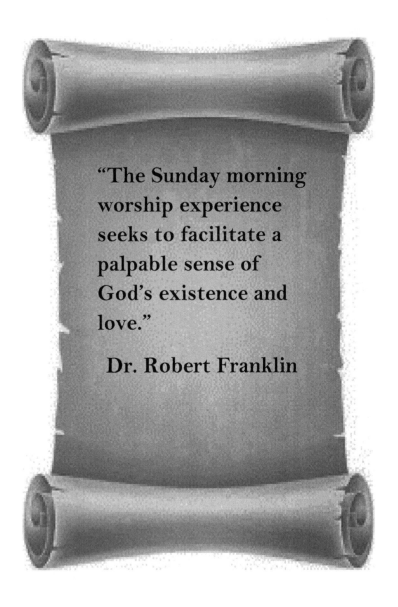

"The Sunday morning worship experience seeks to facilitate a palpable sense of God's existence and love."

Dr. Robert Franklin

One of the great Scriptures that addresses the power of the worship experience, is in the New Testament book of Acts:

> "About midnight Paul and Silas were praying and singing hymns to God, and the prisoners were listening to them, and suddenly there was a great earthquake, so that the foundations of the prison were shaken. And immediately all the doors were opened, and everyone's bonds were unfastened. When the jailer woke and saw that the prison doors were open, he drew his sword and was about to kill himself, supposing that the prisoners had escaped. But Paul cried with a loud voice, "Do not harm yourself, for we are all here." And the jailer called for lights and rushed in, and trembling with fear he fell down before Paul and Silas. Then he brought them out and said, "Sirs, what must I do to be saved?" And they said, "Believe in the Lord Jesus, and you will be saved, you and your household."
> (Acts 16:25-31)

Preachers love this story! I have heard preachers rift on how Paul and Silas turned their cell into a sanctuary, how they turned the prison into a place of praise, and how they turned a jailhouse into a church house and held a midnight revival. As a preacher, I too have rifted on how Paul and Silas had the jailhouse rocking! But what I personally love about this story, is that it points to what a spirit filled, powerful worship experience can and will accomplish.

A powerful worship experience will set people free. A great worship experience positions God's people to be set free from the chains and shackles that bind them. On any given Sunday, people arrive at our churches weighed down and bound by the trials and tribulations in their lives. But when they come into the sanctuary and have the opportunity to lift up their hands, sing songs of praise and thanksgiving, and turn their attention towards God, they encounter the liberating Spirit of God. The Apostle Paul makes this truth clear in the Epistle of 2 Corinthians, for it is there where he declares, "where the Spirit of the Lord is, there is freedom" (2 Cor. 3:17).

While a powerful worship experience will set people free, it will also position people to be saved. Jesus said, "And I, when I am lifted up from the earth, will draw all people to myself." (Jn. 12:32). The Sunday morning worship experience is an opportunity to lift up Jesus. The songs that we sing, the sermons that we preach, and the praise that we render should lift up the saving reality of Jesus in some form or fashion. In the Acts text, the worship experience in that prison cell paved the way for the jailor and his entire family to be saved. This is the power of the Sunday morning worship experience. During worship, the redemptive power of the Spirit meets people where they are and invites them into a saving relationship with Jesus Christ.

When the Salt Losses its Saltiness

Jesus reminds us that we are "the salt of the earth" (Matt. 5:13). Yet, when salt losses its saltiness, Jesus says that it is "no longer good for anything except to be thrown out". In the ancient world and even today, salt is a useful and effective compound. However, when salt breaks down, it loses its usefulness and effectives. I believe this metaphor is helpful when describing the Sunday morning worship experience. The overall worship experience must be "salty"; it must be effective in regards to inspiring, edifying and encouraging God's people. But if we fail to do all that we can to keep our worship experiences salty, the Sunday morning service will lose its effectiveness.

In an online article, author Jamie Brown provides an interesting critique of today's worship celebrations. Brown argues that "the theme of "performancism" is becoming a problem. He suggests that the "the worship leader as the performer, the congregation as the audience, and the sanctuary as the concert hall"[2] is becoming problematic. To be sure, the Sunday morning worship service of many congregations look very much like a concert – strobe and spot lights, large bands, dancers, praise teams, etc. While I personally do not have issues with the more contemporary styles of worship, I have encountered pastors and church leaders who are obsessively concerned with the staging, lighting, and "production" of the service, believing that the "performance" is what makes the service effective. It seems as if the focus of too many pastors is on entertaining the people, as opposed to transforming the people, through the worship experience.

While "performancism" is becoming a problem in regards to today's Sunday morning worship experience, what is an even more pervasive problem is traditionalism. Many churches have become so set in their Sunday morning rituals and routines that they fail to consider the various elements that foster and facilitate an effective worship experience. For example, do visitors feel welcome when they arrive at your worship service? Did the service start on time; did it drag on too long? Lastly, are the children sleeping in the pews because no part of the Sunday service is geared toward them? When we become so rigid and set in our traditions, we often miss the fact that our total worship experience is missing the mark.

What About Your Worship Experience?

There is an old saying among Baptist preachers: "Good church makes good Christians". The word "church" in the saying is referring to the Sunday morning service. In other words, a good worship service makes a good Christian. So is your ministry having "good church"? Is the total worship experience effective? Take a moment to write down what a visitor would experience (from the parking lot to the pew) on a Sunday morning at your church:

_____

_____

_____

_____

_____

_____

_____

_____

_____

_____

_____

_____

_____

_____

_____

_____

_____

_____

_____

_____

_____

_____

To get a more qualitative analysis of your church's worship experience, answer the following questions:

Circle your response:

1. Do Not Agree

2. Somewhat Agree

3. Agree

4. Strongly Agree

5. Not Applicable

Worship Experience

Greeters are in position to welcome people to worship

1 2 3 4 5

The worship service consistently starts on time

1 2 3 4 5

The sound system is appropriate (not too loud or too low)

1 2 3 4 5

The lighting is appropriate (not too dim or dark)

1 2 3 4 5

Visitors are always welcomed and acknowledged

1 2 3 4 5

There is an organized and planned flow to the worship service

1 2 3 4 5

Your music is uplifting, lively, and inspiring

1 2 3 4 5

You cultivate an atmosphere for people to freely worship

1 2 3 4 5

Your children are included in the worship; efforts are made to
minister to them as well

1 2 3 4 5

The sermons are consistently well developed and relevant

1 2 3 4 5

There is an opportunity during service for "corporate" prayer

1 2 3 4 5

There is an opportunity during service for "corporate" fellowship

1 2 3 4 5

What are the best aspects of your total Worship Experience?

_____

_____

_____

_____

_____

_____

_____

_____

_____

What areas are ripe for improvement?

_____

_____

_____

_____

_____

_____

_____

_____

What changes would you like to make to your Worship experience in the next twelve months?

_____

_____

_____

_____

_____

_____

At my church, we have a monthly New Disciples (i.e. New Members) class. During the class, we often go around the room and ask the new members what brought them to our church, and what led them to join our fellowship. During one of the classes, a young woman stood up and said that it was the "total" experience that led her to join our church. She talked about how people greeted her with a "good morning" in the parking lot and when she entered the church. She talked about how she felt welcomed and how she felt the love of the people. She talked about how the praise and worship ushered her into the presence of the Lord, and how the preached Word fed her soul. And lastly, she talked about how thankful she was that there was age-appropriate services and activities for her children.

This is the essence of what a total worship experience looks like. The total worship experience is concerned with all aspects of the Sunday morning service. It is concerned with assuring that the people feel welcomed and that they experience a sense of Christian fellowship. It is concerned with feeding the mind and the spirit. It is concerned with excellence from the parking lot to the pew. And, when we are concerned with the total worship experience, we enable God's people to wholly experience God's presence and God's love.

In closing, consider this. In his book *Engaging With God: A Biblical Theology of Worship*, David Peterson points out that in the Greek Bible, the verb "to worship" is often translated as "*latreuein*".[3] He goes on to say that the use of this word in non-biblical and biblical literature is often in the context of service; that it speaks to the service that we render unto God. I believe that a great way for pastors and church leaders to worship and render service to God is to do all that we can to foster and facilitate a great worship experience for God's people. Let us do all that we can to ensure that the Sunday morning worship experience is "salty" and effective. For according to Acts 16:25-31, when the worship is right, people will be set free and saved.

Study Questions

1. What is your main take away from this chapter?

2. What is your interpretation of the prison worship scene in Acts 16? Does this scene influence the worship experience at your church in any way? If so, how?

3. What do you think a person would say if he or she were asked why they joined your church? What draws people to your ministry?

Chapter 6

Better Servant-Leaders

"If anyone would be first, he must be last of all and
servant of all."
(Mark 9:35)

Better Servant-Leaders

I learned a long time ago that the most important resource in any church is its people. Without people, there can be no ministry. Without people, there can be no fellowship. Without people, there can be no discipleship. When Jesus started His earthly ministry, He called twelve men to be His disciples. Eleven of those men would ultimately be used by God to establish the church of Jesus Christ.

Disciples were central to the ministry of Jesus. As Jesus prepared His followers for the ministry that was ahead them, He taught and encouraged them to be servant-leaders. Consider the following:

> "Jesus called them to him and said, "You know that the rulers of the Gentiles lord it over them, and their great ones exercise authority over them. It shall not be so among you. But whoever would be great among you must be your servant, and whoever would be first among you must be your slave, even as the Son of Man came not to be served but to serve, and to give his life as a ransom for many." (Matt. 20:25-28)

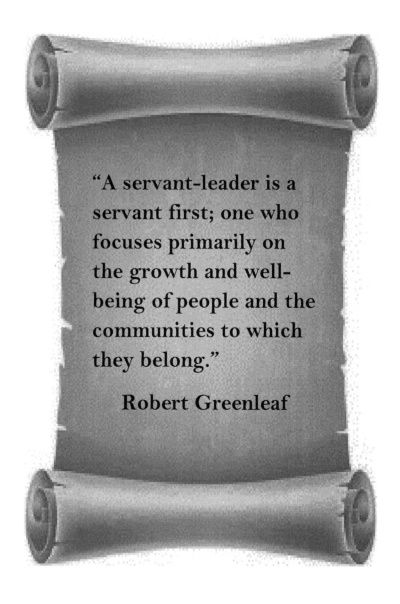

"A servant-leader is a servant first; one who focuses primarily on the growth and well-being of people and the communities to which they belong."

Robert Greenleaf

This Scripture captures the essence of what it means to be a servant-leader. It means that one's focus is on serving and not being served. Robert Greenleaf defines a servant-leader as a "servant first"; as one who "focuses primarily on the growth and well-being of people and the communities to which they belong."[1] Servant-leaders are not those who selfishly pursue power, privilege, or material possessions. Rather, they seek to put the needs of others first and help God's people grow and develop into the disciples that Jesus calls us to be.

What Is Your Mission?

When discussing servant-leadership, it is important to also discuss mission. The role of the servant-leader is to serve people in the context and pursuit of an established mission. Jesus established the mission for His disciples:

> "Go therefore and make disciples of all nations, baptizing them in the name of the Father and of the Son and of the Holy Spirit, teaching them to observe all that I have commanded you. And behold, I am with you always, to the end of the age." (Matt. 28:19-20)

The Disciples were tasked with carrying out the mission as identified in Matthew 28. Servant-leadership was the "how" or the manner in which they were to carry out their mission. They were to serve God's people by baptizing, teaching, and leading them to Christ. What is the vision and mission of your church? What are you looking for your servant-leaders to accomplish as it relates to your ministry? Take a moment to write down the vision and mission of your church.

_____

_____

_____

_____

_____

_____

_____

_____

_____

_____

_____

_____

_____

_____

Knowing the vision and mission of your church, and the vision and mission of each ministry within your church, will help your leaders carry out their respective assignments. For example, if the mission of your Youth Ministry is to establish a foundation that builds character and commitment to Christ, then your leaders will know what they are seeking to accomplish. Moreover, the mission will give you a means to evaluate the effectiveness of your leaders and discern where more training and attention is required.

Temptations

An experienced and "seasoned" preacher once told me to be mindful of temptations, because if you are not careful temptations will pull you away from where God would have you to be. When it comes to our servant-leaders, temptations can pull them from where God would have them to be as well, specifically the temptations of pride and power. We have all seen prideful leaders. We have all crossed paths with those who have elevated opinions of themselves, and who continually seek out positions of visibility, prestige, and honor. The temptation of pride has a crippling effect because it corrupts the motivations of the leader. Instead of leading to help others, the prideful leader may assume positions of leadership only to receive accolades and applause. Yet, Jesus rejected pride and stressed that leaders must clothe themselves in humility:

"Then Jesus said to the crowds and to his disciples, "The scribes and the Pharisees sit on Moses' seat, so do and observe whatever they tell you, but not the works they do. For they preach, but do not practice. They tie up heavy burdens, hard to bear, and lay them on people's shoulders, but they themselves are not willing to move them with their finger. They do all their deeds to be seen by others. For they make their phylacteries broad and their fringes long, and they love the place of honor at feasts and the best seats in the synagogues and greetings in the marketplaces and being called rabbi by others......The greatest among you shall be your servant. Whoever exalts himself will be humbled, and whoever humbles himself will be exalted." (Matt. 23:1-7;11-23)

While the temptation of pride can be debilitating, the temptation of power will also have a crippling effect on servant-leaders. The great Henry Nouwen argues that the "greatest irony of the church is that its leaders constantly give in to the temptation of power."[2] The intoxicating effects of power can encourage behaviors that cause serious ruptures in the community of faith. Infighting, schisms, the unwillingness to share information or compromise, and the need to be "right" are often motivated by the desire to maintain or exercise power. But Jesus taught the Disciples to rethink the idea of power when He served notice that the first shall be last:

"And they came to Capernaum. And when he was in the house he asked them, "What were you discussing on the way?" But they kept silent, for on the way they had argued with one another about who was the greatest. And he sat down and called the twelve. And he said to them, "If anyone would be first, he must be last of all and servant of all." (Mar. 9:33-35)

As pastors and leaders, we must do as Jesus did: we must teach our servant-leaders to become better leaders. We must invest time and effort in them. We must invest resources in them, for as they become better, the people they lead will become better. Through training, our goal should be to develop servant-leaders who submit themselves to the leadership, vision and mission of the church in word and in deed. Moreover, we should work with our leaders so that they use the power and authority entrusted to them to serve others. Lastly, we must teach our leaders (through study and personal example) to emulate the example of Jesus Christ as they look beyond their personal interests to the interests of others.

What About Your Servant-Leaders?

Servant-leaders are a gift to the church. Through the work that they do for the church, they inspire and enliven the potential of those around them. So what about your servant-leaders? Take a moment to write down some of the things that you are currently doing to make your leaders better:

_____

_____

_____

_____

_____

_____

_____

_____

_____

_____

_____

_____

_____

_____

_____

_____

To get a more qualitative analysis of how you may be helping your servant-leaders to become better leaders, answer the following questions:

Circle your response:

1. Do Not Agree
2. Somewhat Agree
3. Agree
4. Strongly Agree
5. Not Applicable

Servant-Leaders

You hold regular meetings with your leaders

1 2 3 4 5

You provide training opportunities specifically for your leaders

1 2 3 4 5

You establish criteria for who can serve in leadership roles

1 2 3 4 5

You share your expectations for leadership at your church

1 2 3 4 5

You have a mission statement in place for each of your ministries

1 2 3 4 5

You regularly evaluate the effectiveness of your leaders and provide feedback

1 2 3 4 5

You provide multiple opportunities for Bible Study

1 2 3 4 5

You require your leaders to attend Bible study

1 2 3 4 5

You provide periodic workshops for personal growth and development

1 2 3 4 5

You are intentional about assessing the spiritual gifts of your leaders

1 2 3 4 5

You frequently pray with and for your leaders

1 2 3 4 5

You thank and recognize your leaders often for their service

1 2 3 4 5

What do you appreciate most about your current leaders?

_____

_____

_____

_____

_____

_____

_____

_____

_____

What are some areas of improvement for your current leaders?

_____

_____

_____

_____

_____

_____

_____

What leadership changes do you plan to make in the next 12 months?

_____

_____

_____

_____

_____

_____

_____

_____

Several years ago, the question "What Would Jesus Do," represented by the acronym WWJD, began to appear on tee-shirts, bracelets, and various paraphernalia. The idea of the campaign was to cause the wearers of the paraphernalia to consider the person and example of Jesus Christ in their actions and decisions. Yet, one would have to agree that it is hard to know what Jesus would do without first knowing what Jesus did. What Jesus did, from a leadership perspective, was to exemplify a servant-leadership model; a model that prioritized the needs of others, and focused on the growth and well-being of God's people

In the Gospel of John, we find the narrative where Jesus washes the feet of the twelve. In so doing, He admonishes them to do likewise saying:

"If I then, your Lord and Teacher, have washed your feet, you also ought to wash one another's feet. For I have given you an example, that you also should do just as I have done to you." (Jn. 13:14-15).

This is the example that we must teach our leaders to follow. We must teach them to serve the people in our ministries as Jesus serves us. So let us commit to investing time and resources into our servant-leaders. Let us commit to praying for them regularly, and letting them know how much we appreciate them frequently. Let us commit to doing all that we can to make our leaders better.

Study Questions

1. What is your main take away from this chapter?

2. How do you interpret Mark 9:33-35, and how could you use this Scripture to train your servant-leaders?

3. Do you have written standards for your leaders? What are your standards? Would you remove a leader for violating your standards or would you focus on training he or she more?

Chapter 7

Better Messaging

"Write the vision; make it plain on tablets, so he may run who reads it."

(Habakkuk 2:2)

Better Messaging

In July of 2018, I attended a workshop called "SucessQuest", facilitated by the great Dr. Chike Akua.[1] During the workshop, Dr. Akua reminded us that we have a responsibility and an obligation to share what God has given us. In other words, there is a song in us that somebody needs to hear. There is a book in us that somebody needs to read. There is a workshop in us that somebody needs to attend. There is knowledge in us that somebody needs to receive. According to Dr. Akua, God has blessed us with vision, knowledge, experience, wisdom, and a message for the masses, and it is our divine responsibility and obligation to share what God has given us.

This notion of having an obligation to share what we have was reiterated in a blog that I recently read. The subject of the blog post was "How To Get Your Message Heard".[2] However, as the author talked about getting your message heard, the following observation was shared: "If you have an empowering message to share, it is your responsibility to share it with the world. The universe wants to use you as a vessel, go with it, fearlessly share your voice, in a powerful and inspiring way." In a very real sense, the author is reminding us that we have an obligation to share our message with the world.

"If you have an empowering message to share, it is your responsibility to share it with the world."

simpleluxeliving.com

You Have A Testimony

It is safe to suggest that the reason you are in ministry is because God has a call on your life. God has given you something to say about Jesus; God has given you a testimony. You have seen the Lord move in your life. You have experienced His grace and mercy. You know, first hand, the transformative power of His love. God has given you a testimony, a message to share with those far and near. It is the message of the Gospel, and it is a message that God wants to use you to tell.

Consider the story of the demon possessed man from the land of the Gerasenes:

> "Then they sailed to the country of the Gerasenes which is opposite Galilee. When Jesus had stepped out on land, there met him a man from the city who had demons. For a long time he had worn no clothes, and he had not lived in a house but among the tombs. When he saw Jesus, he cried out and fell down before him and said with a loud voice, "What have you to do with me, Jesus, Son of the Most High God? I beg you, do not torment me." For he had commanded the unclean spirit to come out of the man. (For many a time it had seized him. He was

kept under guard and bound with chains and shackles, but he would break the bonds and be driven by the demon into the desert.) Jesus then asked him, "What is your name?" And he said, "Legion," for many demons had entered him. And they begged him not to command them to depart into the abyss. Now a large herd of pigs was feeding there on the hillside, and they begged him to let them enter these. So he gave them permission. Then the demons came out of the man and entered the pigs, and the herd rushed down the steep bank into the lake and drowned."

"The man from whom the demons had gone begged that he might be with him, but Jesus sent him away, saying, "Return to your home, and declare how much God has done for you." And he went away, proclaiming throughout the whole city how much Jesus had done for him." (Lk. 8:26-33;38-39)

A close read of the text makes it clear that the man had a testimony. He had met Jesus for himself. Jesus met him at a low point in his life. When Jesus found him, he was naked and demon possessed. But when Jesus left him, he was clothed and loosed from the demons that had him bound. However, the relevant portion of the story is what happened after the man was delivered from his demons. Jesus instructs him to go and declare "how much God has done for you".

The man had a message. And according to the text, he went on to proclaim that message throughout his city.

Likewise, you have a message. God has blessed you with a ministry, and through your ministry you have an obligation to share your message far and wide. Like the man in the text, Jesus is urging you to share your message throughout your city. For example, your youth ministry is doing great things with the youth at your church, and somebody needs to know it. Or maybe you have a Women's Ministry that is empowering women, or a Men's Ministry that is helping men become better husbands and fathers, or a Prison Ministry that is helping and encouraging those who are incarcerated. If this is the case, somebody needs to know it. So, it is incumbent upon you to do all that you can to get your message to reach as many people as possible.

What About Your Messaging?

The Bible reminds us to "write the vision; make it plain on tablets, so he may run who reads it" (Hab. 2:2). A simple interpretation of this text is that God has given the vision. But it is the responsibility of the recipient of the vision to cast the vision clearly, so that those who read it can run with it. Your vision and your message has to be cast so that people (near and far) can catch it and run with it.

So how are you doing with your messaging? Take a moment to write down some of the ways in which you are currently messaging your ministry:

_____

_____

_____

_____

_____

_____

_____

_____

_____

_____

_____

_____

_____

_____

_____

_____

_____

_____

_____

_____

_____

To get a more qualitative analysis of how you are messaging your ministry, answer the following questions:

Circle your response:

1. Do Not Agree

2. Somewhat Agree

3. Agree

4. Strongly Agree

5. Not Applicable

Messaging

You currently have a presence on social media: Facebook, Twitter, Instagram, YouTube, etc.

1 2 3 4 5

Your church has a website that shares current information and upcoming events

1 2 3 4 5

You frequently share pictures and video clips via your media platforms

1 2 3 4 5

Your church is live streaming Worship services, Bible studies, and special events

1 2 3 4 5

You have a welcome packet for your visitors

1 2 3 4 5

You collect information about your visitors and share ongoing information with them

1 2 3 4 5

You have a "logo" that appears on all of your messaging

1 2 3 4 5

Your branding is consistent across all of your publications and messaging

1 2 3 4 5

Your publications and materials look professional

1 2 3 4 5

You have a tagline that conveys what your ministry is about

1 2 3 4 5

What do you like most about how you are currently messaging your ministry?

_____

_____

_____

_____

_____

_____

_____

_____

What are some areas of improvement for your messaging?

_____

_____

_____

_____

_____

_____

_____

_____

What messaging changes do you plan to make in the next twelve months?

_____

_____

_____

_____

_____

_____

_____

_____

In Luke's Gospel, we are introduced to the "Women at the Well". The Bible tells the story of how a Samaritan woman meets Jesus at Jacob's well. The encounter was so profound and transformative that the woman was compelled to drop everything that she was doing, and go share her experience with those in her town:

> "So the woman left her water jar and went away into town and said to the people, "Come, see a man who told me all that I ever did. Can this be the Christ?" They went out of the town and were coming to Him." (Lk. 4:28-30)

The woman apparently reached many people with her message. So much so that the people left the town with the expressed intent to go and meet Jesus. And because of the woman's message, many people came to believe in Jesus, for the Bible says that "Many Samaritans from that town believed in Him because of the woman's testimony" (v. 39).

This is why you need to be sure that your message is reaching the masses. Somebody will come to believe in Jesus because of your ministry and your message. Lives will be transformed, souls will be saved, and God's people will be served through your church. So, be sure that you are doing all that you can to make your messaging better; be sure that you are doing all that you can to ensure that your message is reaching the masses.

Study Questions

1. What is your main take away from this chapter?

2. How can you leverage the story of the Woman at the Well (Luke 4) to encourage your ministry to do more as it relates to reaching a greater number of people in your city with your message?

3. Have you ever thought that your message should reach audiences around the world? If so, what steps can you take to make it happen?

Chapter 8

So Now What?

"But be doers of the word, and not hearers only."

(James 1:22)

So Now What?

An old friend used to share a funny story about his nephew's graduation. As the story goes, my friend's family had gathered to celebrate the college graduation of his nephew Paul. After the graduation, Paul and a few of his friends had gathered outside of the auditorium to take pictures. As they posed for the pictures, an old wino staggered into the group in an effort to get in the picture. As they shooed and pushed him away, the indignant and intoxicated old man turned to them, and with slurred speech, he yelled out: "Congratulations! But what ya'll gonna do now?"

Allow me to say "Congratulations"! Over the last few chapters, you have learned some practical steps on how you can make your ministry better. You have learned how to make your buildings and grounds better, your ministries and programs better, your worship experience better, your servant-leaders better, and your messaging better. You have reflected on certain areas of your ministry, and you have been challenged to think about your ministry in some new ways. But the question is, so now what? Echoing the old man at the graduation, "what ya'll gonna do now?

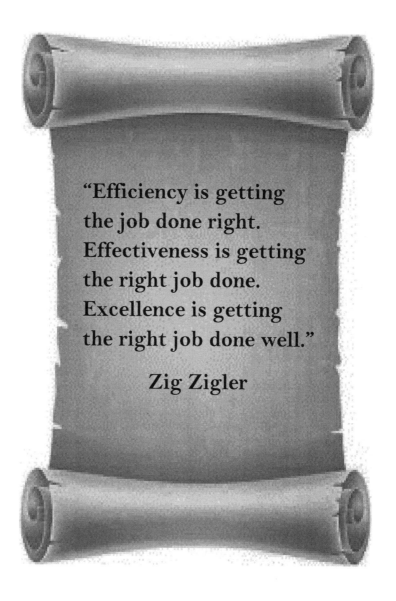

"Efficiency is getting
the job done right.
Effectiveness is getting
the right job done.
Excellence is getting
the right job done well."

Zig Zigler

The Hope

My hope is that you embrace what you have learned and take action. My hope is that you move beyond the status quo and believe that things can and will be better at your church. My hope is that you expand your thinking beyond this book and look for additional ways to improve your ministry. My hope is that you adopt a spirit of excellence that motivates you to continue to evaluate your ministry long after you put this book down. Author Zig Zigler reminds us that "efficiency is getting the job done right. Effectiveness is getting the right job done. Excellence is getting the right job done well."[1] This is my hope, that excellence will become a part of your ministerial DNA, such that everything you do in your ministry is done well.

However, two hazards exist that could truly hinder your efforts to better your ministry. The first is familiarity. Sometimes we are so close to, and familiar with, our ministry that we cannot see what needs to be improved. I have a picture in my kitchen that has been there since I moved into my house six years ago. It is so familiar to me, that I often do not pay attention to it. I recently had a guest in my home, and my guest pointed out that the picture was actually crooked. I had not noticed it. It had become so familiar that I could not see that it needed some attention.

The second hazard is immobility. There are times when we become so overwhelmed by all of the work that needs to be done, that we become stagnant and immobile. A few years ago, a friend asked me to help him move. When I arrived at his house the night before the move, I noticed a bunch of empty boxes. He had not yet begun to pack up his things. I asked him why so many boxes were still empty. He said that there was so much to do that he did not know where to start. Every time he started to move, the magnitude of the work at hand overwhelmed him and caused him to stand still.

If you think about it, both of these hazards can be avoided if you get some help. In truth, you need to assemble a *Better Before Bigger* team. This team will not only help you see what you may not be able to see, but also help you prioritize and manage the changes that need to be made in your ministry. You may consider using the following phased-approach in regards to forming your *Better Before Bigger* team:

Phase I – Centering

This phase involves grounding the team in a theology of "*Better*". Specifically, in this phase you will identify the volunteers who will participate on the team, and establish the frequency of your meetings. This phase also includes sharing the vision and mission of the team, and sharing your thoughts and action items from your journey through this book.

Phase II – Choosing

This phase involves identifying the specific areas to be improved, and identifying the timeframe in which these improvements will be made (i.e. within the next six months). The team may choose to identify at least one area for improvement in the five areas of focus: buildings and grounds, ministries and programs, worship, servant-leadership, and messaging. This phase will also include the analysis of the resources required to make the identified changes.

Phase III – Constructing

In this phase, the team will construct a plan of action and execute it. The primary goal of this phase is to make the identified changes. This includes organizing the necessary resources and implementing the change. For example, if the plan is to launch a new church website, this is the phase in which the website designer is identified, the website is designed, and the website actually goes live.

Phase IV – Critiquing

In this last phase, the team will critique and evaluate the success and effectiveness of the implemented changes. Did the changes really make the ministry better? Did the changes deliver the desired effect? For example, if the team decided to implement online streaming for your worship services, how many people are watching the stream? Is the stream helping you reach a wider audience with your message? If not, then the team may have to return to Phase III and develop a new plan of action.

Who Should Be On Your Team?

In the Fall of 2016, I preached a sermon series entitled "Who's On Your Team"? The gist of the series is that God has a purpose and a plan for all of us. There are blessings and new horizons that God has in store for us, and those around you (those on your team) will either hurt you or help you as it relates to taking hold of all that God has for you. I believe that the same is true in terms of whom you select to work on your *Better Before Bigger* Team. You should have people on your team who not only can help the ministry, but also those who have a vested and passionate interest in seeing the ministry flourish.

In the sermon series, I focused on the Biblical characters who were on "Team Jesus". I believe that the "type" of people who were on the Lord's team are the type of people that you should have on your team. For example, you need a "John the Baptist" on your team. You need someone who is frank and honest, and not afraid to call things as they are and say what needs to be said:

> "He said therefore to the crowds that came out to be baptized by him, "You brood of vipers! Who warned you to flee from the wrath to come? Bear fruits in keeping with repentance. And do not begin to say to yourselves, 'We have Abraham as our father.' For I tell you, God is able from these stones to raise up children for Abraham. Even now the axe is laid to the root of the trees. Every tree therefore that does not bear good fruit is cut down and thrown into the fire." (Lk. 3:7-9)

John the Baptist kept it real. He was not afraid to tell the truth. Likewise, you need people on your team who will keep it real with you. Someone with credibility and respect. Someone, for example, who is willing to tell you what you need to hear, and not just what you want to hear. There are some changes that need to be made that may be difficult for you to hear. This is why you need someone on your team who is able to engage in some real talk with you; real talk that you can hear and receive.

You also need a "Mary Magdalene" on your team. Mary had a sincere love for Jesus; a love that was measured not by what she said, but rather by what she did for the Lord: "Now on the first day of the week Mary Magdalene came to the tomb early, while it was still dark" (Jn. 20:1). It was Mary who got up and went to anoint the body of Jesus. There was a stone covering the mouth of the tomb. But Mary went anyhow, believing that somehow she would be able to get to Jesus. And because of her love and effort for Jesus, she was the first to see the risen Savior.

Mary's love and support for Jesus prompted her to make a sacrifice for Jesus. She sacrificed her sleep so that she could go and anoint the body of Jesus. You truly need this type of person on your team. Somebody who has made sacrifices on behalf of your ministry. Someone who has supported the ministry through his or her time, talent, and treasure. Someone who does not just say that they love the church, but who actually demonstrates their love by what they do for the church. It would be a mistake to have someone at the table making decisions for the church, and that person has not demonstrated any real support, or any real tangible sacrifices for the church.

Next, you need a "John" on your team, someone who is trustworthy and responsible. The Apostle John was referred to as the "Beloved" disciple in Scripture. He was a trusted part of the Lord's inner circle, and he was often invited to accompany Jesus to select places. The greatest evidence of John's trustworthiness, however, can be seen at the cross:

> "But standing by the cross of Jesus were his mother and his mother's sister, Mary the wife of Clopas, and Mary Magdalene. When Jesus saw his mother and the disciple whom he loved standing nearby, he said to his mother, "Woman, behold, your son!" Then he said to the disciple, "Behold, your mother!" And from that hour the disciple took her to his own home." (Jn. 19:25-27)

In his dying moments, Jesus entrusted the care of his mother to John. This speaks volumes to the type of man that John was. He was obviously a man of integrity, a man who was trustworthy and responsible. So, be sure that you have a John on your team. Someone who has demonstrated that they are able to handle the responsibilities that you have assigned to them. Someone who is trustworthy and will actually do what they say. The work ahead of you will be daunting and difficult at times, and you will need people around you who are able to get things done.

Lastly, you will need a "Peter" on your team. If you look at the life of Peter, you will discover that he often made mistakes and fell short. Yet, in spite of his shortcomings, Peter is by far the boldest of the twelve disciples. It was Peter, for example, who was willing to get out of the boat and walk on water:

"And in the fourth watch of the night he came to them, walking on the sea. But when the disciples saw him walking on the sea, they were terrified, and said, "It is a ghost!" and they cried out in fear. But immediately Jesus spoke to them, saying, "Take heart; it is I. Do not be afraid." And Peter answered him, "Lord, if it is you, command me to come to you on the water." He said, "Come." So Peter got out of the boat and walked on the water and came to Jesus." (Matt. 14:25-29)

When it gets down to it, you need some bold water-walkers on your team! You need people who are willing to move beyond the safety of the status quo and get out of the boat. There will be those around you who are afraid of change and who will want to stay in the boat. There will be those who will never want to move beyond their comfort zones. But this is why you need a few Peters on your team. People who are willing to trust God and take a risk; who are willing to take the Lord at His Word and take some steps by faith. People who are willing to get out of the boat and walk on the water with you.

In each of the previous chapters, you identified at least one thing that you would like to change over the next twelve months as it relates your buildings and grounds, ministries and programs, worship experience, servant-leaders, and messaging.

I would encourage you to develop a short-term plan. In this plan, your team can work to identify the things that you can make better within the next thirty to sixty days. These are the quick wins that deal with the low hanging fruit; those things that you can change right away without a whole lot of resources. This could include, for example, developing a visitor packet, or launching a Facebook page, or starting a much needed ministry or program.

After working on your short-term plan, turn your attention to a long-term plan. This plan might include those items that require larger amounts of resources. For example, the long-term plan might include painting the exterior of the church or having the parking lot repaired or expanded. It might include investing in high definition cameras so that you can have a high quality stream of your worship service.

Alternatively, it may include an offsite retreat where you and your leaders can escape for training and fellowship. Please note that your long-term plan must not be a "wishful thinking" wish list, but rather a plan of action that you intend to complete in a specified timeframe (i.e. in one year).

Conclusion

In the third chapter of the Epistle of Ephesians, Paul prays for the church (Eph. 3:14-21). He prays that God would strengthen them through the power of His Spirit. He prays that Christ would dwell in their hearts. He prays that they might be rooted and grounded in love, and that they might know the breadth, length, height, and depth of the Lord's love. Lastly, he prays that they might be filled with all the fullness of God. This is my prayer for you and your church. In addition to all that Paul prayed for, I also pray that God will truly bless your ministry to be better; that as you become better, God will bless your ministry to become bigger!

In closing, I leave you with Paul's benediction as recorded in Ephesians 3:20-21:

> "Now to him who is able to do far more abundantly than all that we ask or think, according to the power at work within us, to him be glory in the church and in Christ Jesus throughout all generations, forever and ever. Amen."

Study Questions

1. What is your main take away from this chapter?

2. As you think about the members of your *Better Before Bigger* Team, who comes to mind?

3. What are your short-term plans (thirty to sixty days), and your long-term plans (within twelve months) to better your ministry?

Notes

Get Your Mind Right

[1] https://www.cbsnews.com/news/60-minutes-meet-a-convicted-felon-who-became-a-georgetown-law-professor/

[2] Toler, Stan, Nelson Alan, "The Five Star Church: Serving God and His People with Excellence," (Ventura, CA: Regal Books, 1999), p.##

Better Building & Grounds

[1] https://www.goodreads.com/quotes/7515235-you-never-get-a-second-chance-to-make-a-first

[2] Wind, James P. "Places of Worship: Exploring Their History" (Altamira Press, Walnut Creek CA, 1997), p. 1

Better Ministries & Programs

[1] No Place for Me: I Still Love God, But I've Lost Faith in the Black Church By John W. Fountain, Washington Post, Sunday, July 17, 2005

[2] Boring, M. Eugene, "The New Interpreter's Bible Commentary – Vol. VIII," (Nashville, TN: Abingdon Press, 1994), p. 405

[3] Thomas, Frank, "Soul of the Congregation," (Nashville, TN: Abington Press, 2000), p. 12

Better Worship Experiences

[1] Franklin, Robert M. "Another Day's Journey: Black Churches Confronting the American Crisis," (Minneapolis, MN: Augsburg Fortress Press, 1997), p. 31

[2] https://worthilymagnify.com/2014/05/19/crash/

[3] Peterson, David, "Engaging With God: A Biblical Theology of Worship," (Downers Grove, IL: InterVaristy Press, 1992), p. 64

Better Servant-Leaders

[1] https://www.greenleaf.org/

[2] Henri J.M. Nouwen, "In The Name of Jesus," (New York: Cross, 2002), p 76

Better Messaging

[1] http://www.chikeakua.net/

[2] http://www.simpleluxeliving.com/god-is-my-publicist-how-to-manifest-media-for-your-message/

So Now What?

[1] Toler, Stan, Nelson Alan, "The Five Star Church: Serving God and His People with Excellence," (Ventura, CA: Regal Books, 1999), p.59

Made in the USA
Columbia, SC
21 July 2022